SCIENCE FRONTIERS

BLACK HOLES

AND OTHER BIZARRE SPACE OBJECTS

DAVID JEFFERIS

Crabtree Publishing Company

www.crabtreebooks.com

INTRODUCTION

If you look up at the sky on a dark night, it may seem calm, but space is not as peaceful as it appears.

We live in a universe that is bathed in deadly **radiation.** In space, **stars** are born and die in massive blasts of energy. Black holes are regions of space that are so powerful, they can suck in stars. They are called black holes because light cannot escape from them.

Are black holes a danger to Earth? Where are they located? Find the answer to these questions and more inside this book.

Crabtree Publishing Company
www.crabtreebooks.com

PMB 59051   616 Welland Ave
350 Fifth Ave.   St. Catharines, ON
59th Floor   Canada
New York   L2M 5V6
NY 10118

Edited by
Isabella McIntyre

Coordinating editor
Ellen Rodger

Editors
Rachel Eagen
Adrianna Morganelli

Production Coordinator
Rosie Gowsell

Technical consultant
Mat Irvine FBIS

Created and produced by
David Jefferis/BuzzBooks

©2006 David Jefferis/BuzzBooks

Printed in Canada/012013/DM20121114

Library of Congress Cataloging-in-Publication Data
Jefferis, David.
  Black holes and other bizarre space objects / written by David Jefferis.
    p. cm. -- (Science frontiers)
  Includes bibliographical references and index.
  ISBN-13: 978-0-7787-2856-6 (rlb)
  ISBN-10: 0-7787-2856-0 (rlb.)
  ISBN-13: 978-0-7787-2870-2 (pbk.)
  ISBN-10: 0-7787-2870-6 (pbk.)
    1. Black holes (Astronomy)--Juvenile literature. 2. Stars--Juvenile literature. I. Title.
  QB843.B55J44 2006
  23.8'875--dc22
                2005035761
                   LC

Library and Archives Canada Cataloging-in-Publication
CIP available at Library and Archives Canada

Pictures on these pages, clockwise from above left:

1 The XMM-Newton space telescope soon after its launch.
2 A black hole, surrounded by a glowing circle of gases.
3 A new black hole sends out a burst of energy into space.
4 Material from a big, cool star is sucked into a tiny companion star.

CONTENTS

WHAT IS A BLACK HOLE?

A black hole is an object with gravity so strong that light cannot escape from it. This lack of light makes the black hole invisible in space.

▲ A cloud of gas is left after a star explodes. A black hole is thought to be in the middle.

Black holes are thought to be the last stage in the life of a star. For most of a star's life, there is a balance between the force of **gravity** trying to collapse the star and the outward, explosive forces that make the star so hot. When a star's fuel is used up, gravity takes over. The star's core collapses, then explodes. The energy and matter left behind is so massive and so **dense** that even light cannot escape from this region of space. It becomes more compressed until a black hole is born.

▶ The big star's outer layers are being sucked away by a nearby black hole. The gases glow as they fall towards it.

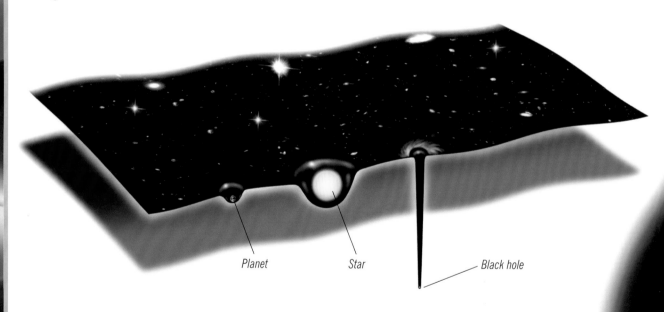

Planet   Star   Black hole

The new black hole is a very strange object. It has all the matter of the original star's core material squeezed into a single point. The black hole's gravity is intense, but luckily it affects only a localized, or small, area of space, so it cannot swallow up the entire universe.

▲ Here, space is depicted as a rubbery sheet where objects sink into holes, or wells of gravity. Planets are less massive than stars, so they do not sink in as deeply. A black hole is like a bottomless hole in space.

BIRTH OF A BLACK HOLE

This is how scientists think a black hole forms at the end of a star's lifetime.

1 A big star glows steadily for billions of years, using hydrogen as fuel in a burning process called nuclear fusion.

2 As the star ages, it expands, in size.

3 Eventually, the star collapses when its fuel is used up.

The outer layers are blown off in a massive explosion called a supernova. The star's core continues to collapse and shrink.

4 The core keeps on getting smaller and denser until it forms a black hole.

At this point, the black hole disappears from view. Although invisible, the black hole continues to suck in, or attract, material nearby.

Gases form a disk as they spiral into the black hole.

SINGULARITY AND DISK

Nobody has actually seen a black hole. To identify one, scientists look for evidence such as stars being pulled into the black hole.

▲ Karl Schwarzschild was a German scientist in the 1900s, whose theory on how black holes operate is called the Schwarzschild Radius.

Scientists have some theories of how black holes work. The gravitational pull of a black hole draws matter towards the center where it is destroyed. The center is a region where the ordinary rules of science do not apply. This area is called a **singularity**. Surrounding the singularity is a boundary called the event horizon. This is the place where objects are drawn into the black hole.

► Black holes have features that include the singularity (1) and event horizon (2). They may also have an accretion disk (3) and energy jet (4).

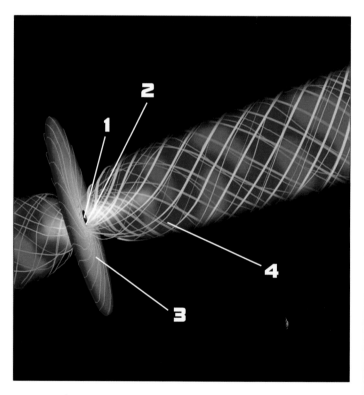

Outside the event horizon there is often a swirling disk of gas and dust called an **accretion disk**. This gas and dust is pulled into the black hole. Scientists believe energy from gases form glowing jets or streams of light that pour out of the black hole. The glowing jets are one clue that scientists use to identify black holes.

When scientists see images of space that show these glowing jets of light surrounding an area of blackness, they know they have located a black hole. For example, the picture below shows a large bubble of pink gas. It is blown across space by material spun off of a black hole's accretion disk. The black hole is hidden behind the white glow of the disk.

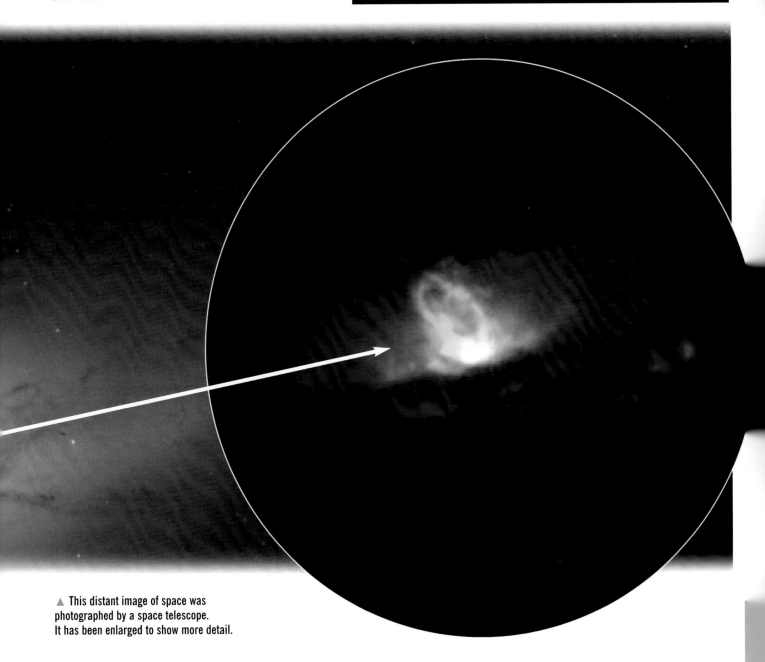

▲ This distant image of space was photographed by a space telescope. It has been enlarged to show more detail.

BLACK HOLE HUNTERS

There are several ways scientists hunt for black holes. They use powerful telescopes that can take pictures of planets, stars, and galaxies **that are millions of miles away.**

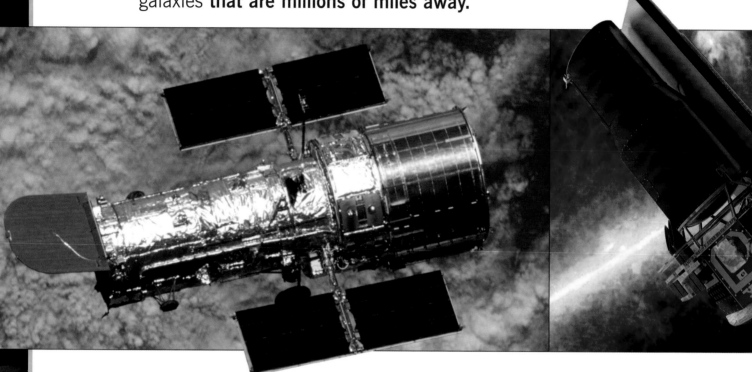

▲ The Hubble Space Telescope was launched in 1990. It has made many discoveries since that time.

The best way to see things in distant space is to use a telescope that can cruise far above the Earth's **atmosphere**. This is because shifting air currents and dust may blur images from even the best ground-based telescopes. One of the first powerful space telescopes was the Hubble, which has taken thousands of pictures of space objects, from nearby **planets** to far-off galaxies.

▲ The Spitzer space telescope was launched in 2003. This high-tech telescope is 33.5 inches (0.85 meters) across.

► Chandra has spotted many distant space objects, including black holes, since it was launched in 1999.

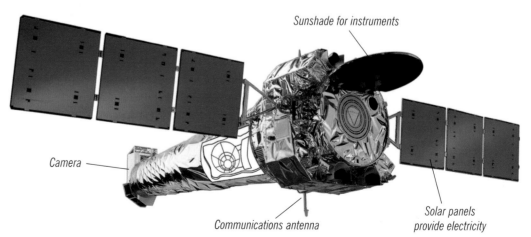

Sunshade for instruments

Camera

Communications antenna

Solar panels provide electricity

▶ The Swift telescope weighs 3,241 pounds (1,470 kilograms) and was sent into space to look for gamma-ray bursts, or flashes of light energy thought to be made by black holes.

▲ XMM-Newton makes a long, looping path around the Earth. Its furthest point reaches one-third of the way to the Moon.

Space telescopes use visible light, the kind of light radiation that we see with our eyes. They also use instruments that are sensitive to other forms of light energy, including radio waves, heat rays, **ultraviolet rays** and **x-rays**. In hospitals, x-rays are used to photograph bones. The x-ray beams pass through flesh, muscle, and organs. The Chandra space telescope uses x-rays to hunt for objects that would otherwise be hidden from view behind clouds of space dust and gas. Chandra is a big machine. It weighs nearly five tons (4.5 tonnes) and has two sets of **solar panels** that span 64 feet (19.5 meters).

CLEAN FOR FLIGHT?

Designing a space telescope that can run reliably for years without any repairs is difficult. The telescope must be built in a "clean room," a space that is kept free of contaminants such as dust. People who work on the telescope wear masks, coveralls, slippers, and gloves. Just one flake of skin or strand of hair in the wrong place could cause the ultra-delicate electronic systems to burn out.

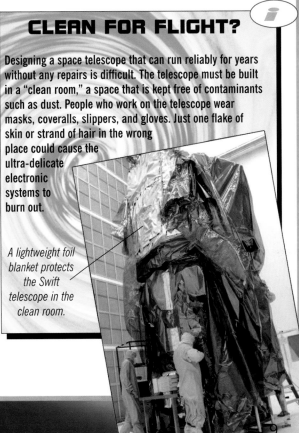

A lightweight foil blanket protects the Swift telescope in the clean room.

WHERE ARE THEY?

Black holes are scattered throughout the universe, although none have ever been discovered anywhere near Earth.

▲ Cygnus X-1 is a double star, or binary pair. The large star (red arrow) feeds a black hole. Cygnus X-1 is about 8,175 light years from Earth.

◀ Scientist Stephen Hawking has written books on black holes and other topics.

The idea that black holes exist has been around for hundreds of years. It was not until the 1970s that **astronomers** thought they actually found one. They saw that the double star Cygnus X-1 gave out more energy than other stars, which is one sign of a black hole.

▶ This telescope image shows the Milky Way galaxy, where a massive black hole is thought to exist.

Cygnus X-1 has two parts. One part is a massive "supergiant" star that is 20 to 30 times bigger than the Sun. Gas and dust from space are pulled toward the supergiant. Scientists believe that the light given off by the gas and dust particles are actually the accretion disk of a black hole.

▲ There are billions and billions of galaxies, extending as far as the most powerful telescopes can see. All of them are thought to contain many black holes.

◄ Galaxies are massive, swirling groups of stars. This one is called the Andromeda galaxy. It has a massive black hole at its heart.

A typical galaxy contains more than 100 billion stars and thousands of black holes.

Quasars are believed to be massive black holes in galaxies more than two billion light years away. A single quasar has more energy than all the stars of an entire galaxy. It is thought that this energy comes from the enormous amount of gas and other material that falls, or is pulled into the accretion disk.

HOW FAR ARE THE STARS?

Space distances are so vast that they are measured in light years, the distance that a ray of light covers in a year, travelling at 186,000 miles per second (300,000 kilometers per second).

A light year is a mind-boggling distance of 5.9 million million miles (9.5 million million kilometers). Shorter distances can be measured in light days, hours, minutes, or seconds. The Sun, for example, is a little more than eight light minutes away.

About 1 million years

About 20,000 years

About 10 million years

▲ It would take a long time for a car, jet, or space probe to travel the distance of a single light year.

11

ENERGY BEAMS

Gamma-ray bursts (GRBs) are the brightest bursts of light that astronomers have ever seen. The energy explosion that marks a GRB is thought to be caused by a black hole.

GRBs are enormous bursts of energy. They are thought to result from massive explosions called **hypernovas**. Hypernovas happen when a massive star collapses to form a black hole and a fireball forms a blasting jet of energy. Hypernovas are usually a series of hiccuping explosions that gradually trail off over several days or weeks.

The energy jet comes from the middle of the GRB

▲ The Swift space telescope was launched in 2004 to observe GRBs. The first GRB was spotted by a Vela satellite in the 1960s.

▶ It is thought that somehow the black hole recharges the energy jet, extending it up to three or four more blasts after the first explosion.

These energy bursts are observed and recorded by satellites that are specially built for the job. The Swift space telescope has three telescopes to observe GRBs and can be pointed in any direction in less than a minute. GRBs are the biggest explosions ever seen. In 1998, a gamma-ray burst lasting only a second or two flashed as bright as the rest of the known universe!

SPECTRUM OF ENERGY

Without light, we could not see the Sun by day or the stars by night. Yet light is only a tiny part of a wide range of energy, called the electromagnetic spectrum (EMS). Different parts of the EMS have different energies, from low-energy radio waves to high-energy gamma rays and cosmic rays.

Space telescopes are built to study all sorts of waves, because high-energy rays can penetrate through space dust, allowing us to get a clear view of things that are not visible in regular light.

Radio waves

Television waves

Microwaves

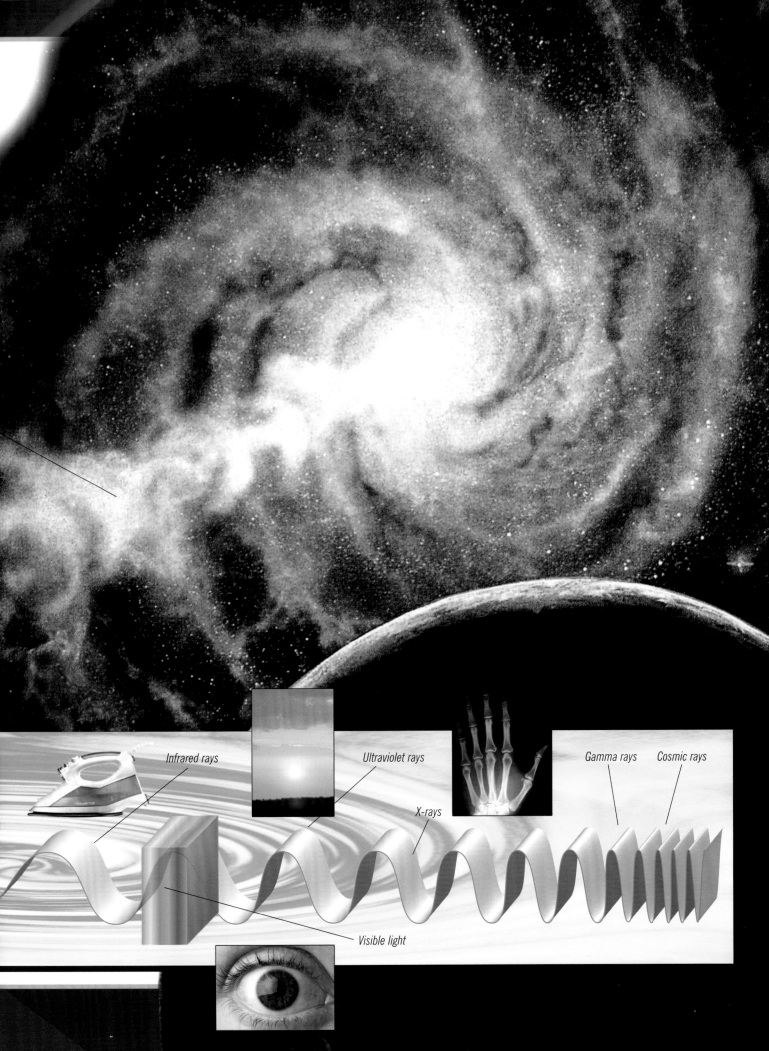

Infrared rays

Ultraviolet rays

Gamma rays   Cosmic rays

X-rays

Visible light

TARGET EARTH?

Astronomers do not think there are any gamma-ray bursts likely to explode near the Earth. They are not sure that there were none in the past, or that there will not be any in the future.

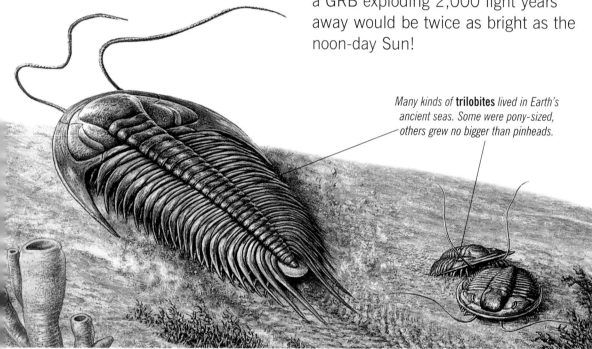

Explosions far away in space seem safe, but what would happen if there was a gamma-ray burst much closer to us? In fact, a GRB would not have to be very close to be visible. It is likely that a GRB exploding 2,000 light years away would be twice as bright as the noon-day Sun!

*Many kinds of **trilobites** lived in Earth's ancient seas. Some were pony-sized, others grew no bigger than pinheads.*

▲ The ozone layer normally protects us from dangerous kinds of space radiation.

▶ If a gamma-ray burst happened close to Earth, it would light up the sky for a few minutes. The energy would strip away much of the Earth's ozone layer, the atmosphere layer that protects the Earth from the Sun's dangerous radiation. Without the ozone layer, the Earth would burn.

▲ Trilobites were among the many sea creatures that died about 450 million years ago.

It is possible that a gamma-ray burst could be a danger as far as 6,000 light years away. Some scientists believe there was a GRB about 450 million years ago. A ten-second blast of gamma rays would have stripped away half of the Earth's ozone layer, which protects us from dangerous radiation.

We know that *something* wiped out much of the world's animal life at that time, but was it a gamma-ray burst? We may never be sure.

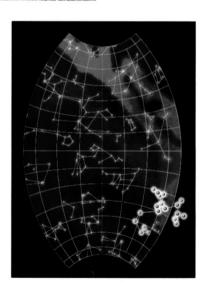

▶ This map shows the Sagittarius star group. Find it on a dark night of star gazing and you are looking towards the nearest black hole in our galaxy.

HOW FAR AWAY IS THE NEAREST BLACK HOLE?

The nearest black hole that researchers have found is about 1,600 light years away. That is quite a distance, although nowhere near the 28,000 light years to the black holes lurking in the middle of our own Milky Way galaxy.

This nearby black hole has no name, and is identified with the star chart number, V4641 Sagittarii, because it lies in the direction of the constellation Sagittarius. It was spotted by astronomers in 1999 when it flared up in a huge burst of x-rays, then faded away again.

V4641's energy bursts seem to be fuelled by gas and dust pouring in from a nearby companion star. The picture at the right shows a bright x-ray burst, which then fades out over about a day as the material is consumed by the black hole.

The brightest part of V4641's x-ray display is shown here in pink and red.

STAR BIRTH

Black holes are not just objects that destroy things near them. They also seem to be behind the creation of many stars and planets.

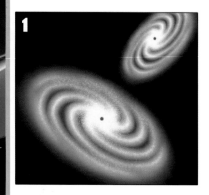

▲ The black hole in Centaurus A is fed by a huge accretion disk. A powerful jet pours out a glowing stream of x-rays and other radiation.

The Centaurus A galaxy is 10 million light years away, making it almost next door to our own galaxy. The images below, taken by the Hubble space telescope, shows where new stars are being formed out of swirling clouds of gas and dust. Centaurus A may not actually be a single galaxy – it could be the result of two galaxies that have collided.

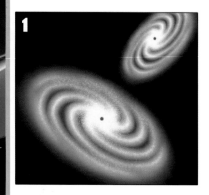
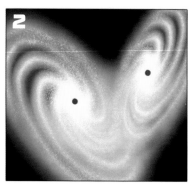
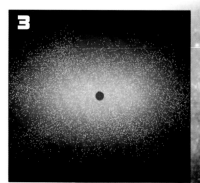

▲ Two galaxies move towards each other (1). They collide (2) and their black holes merge to form one giant black hole (3), surrounded by a huge elliptical galaxy.

Clusters of new stars are shown in blue at the right, while large, swirling clouds of gas and dust glow red and yellow. Other material veils them like smoky curtains. Hidden behind them all is a massive black hole, sucking in matter and pouring out radiation.

New stars

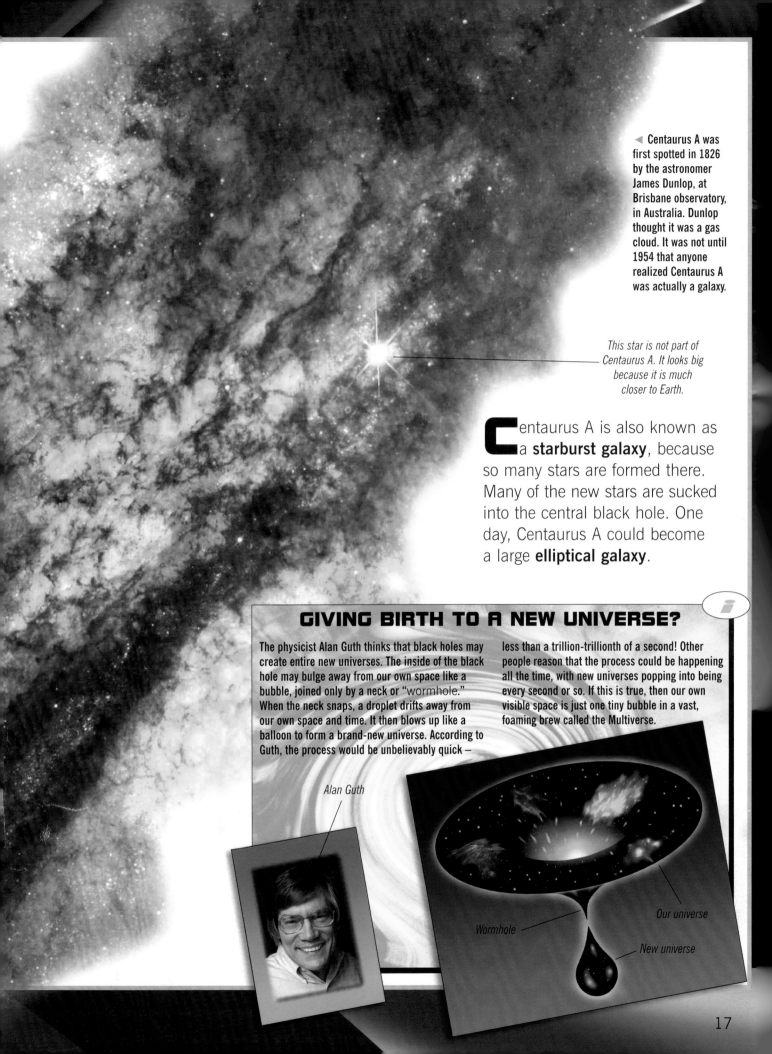

◄ Centaurus A was first spotted in 1826 by the astronomer James Dunlop, at Brisbane observatory, in Australia. Dunlop thought it was a gas cloud. It was not until 1954 that anyone realized Centaurus A was actually a galaxy.

This star is not part of Centaurus A. It looks big because it is much closer to Earth.

Centaurus A is also known as a **starburst galaxy**, because so many stars are formed there. Many of the new stars are sucked into the central black hole. One day, Centaurus A could become a large **elliptical galaxy**.

GIVING BIRTH TO A NEW UNIVERSE?

The physicist Alan Guth thinks that black holes may create entire new universes. The inside of the black hole may bulge away from our own space like a bubble, joined only by a neck or "wormhole." When the neck snaps, a droplet drifts away from our own space and time. It then blows up like a balloon to form a brand-new universe. According to Guth, the process would be unbelievably quick —

less than a trillion-trillionth of a second! Other people reason that the process could be happening all the time, with new universes popping into being every second or so. If this is true, then our own visible space is just one tiny bubble in a vast, foaming brew called the Multiverse.

Alan Guth

Wormhole

Our universe

New universe

17

WORMHOLE HIGHWAYS

Could humans ever travel through a black hole, using it as a tunnel through space?

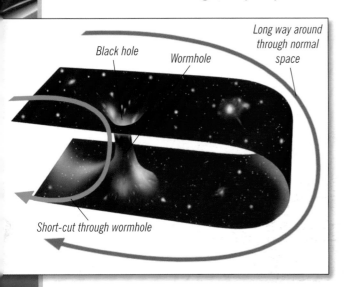

▲ A wormhole transportation system might look like this travel agent's store, offering vacations that need just one step to get there!

Some scientists view black holes as more than just bottomless holes in space. Some astronomers believe black holes are wormholes, or entrances to another point in space and time. Until recently, it was thought that a black hole's gravity would stretch and distort, or change, any object that entered it.

Black hole
Wormhole
Long way around through normal space
Short-cut through wormhole

▶ Here is what future astronauts might see as their spacecraft heads into a wormhole. The hole's huge gravity distorts starlight into shining blurred streaks as the spacecraft passes.

▲ Could a black hole be a tunnel through space with a wormhole connecting two points?

Latest ideas show that entering a large **rotating** black hole might not mean instant doom. Like a wall-of-death ride at a carnival, the outward spinning motion could be enough to balance the gravity pulling you the other way.

▲ Gas explosions on this neutron star, located 25,000 light years from Earth, released more energy in 10 seconds than the Sun produces in a week.

Neutron stars are even smaller than white dwarfs, with a typical size of just 15 miles (25 kilometers) across. They are halfway between a white dwarf and a black hole. A neutron star can gain matter from a surrounding accretion disk. If enough falls in, the neutron star can turn into a black hole.

LIFE ON A NEUTRON STAR?

Could life exist on a neutron star, where you could weigh 67 billion times more than on Earth? The answer is probably not, although we may never find out for sure. But that did not stop scientist Robert L. Forward from trying to determine what creatures could possibly exist in such a strange and exotic environment.

In his novel *Dragon's Egg*, Forward imagined a race of tiny beings he called the Cheela. The Cheela were shaped like pancakes. They lived for just a few minutes.

In the novel, the Cheela were observed developing at lightning speed, by a team of human astronauts. After only a few days, the Cheela went from primitive cave people to an advanced high-tech society!

Dragon's Egg and its sequel, Starquake, were published in the 1980s.

WEIRD WORLDS

Researchers have found many new planets orbiting distant stars. Some of them have three suns, and others have a year that lasts only a few Earth-hours.

How would you like to wake up to see not one, but *three* suns in the sky? That is the view you would get from a planet circling the biggest of a trio of stars in the constellation Cygnus. The planet is located 149 light years from Earth. Normally, the gravity of the other two stars would have cleared away any rocks and dust before they could collect to form planets. Since this was not the case with Cygnus, scientists have been forced to rethink their ideas and develop new theories that explain this phenomenon.

▲ This recently found exoplanet seems to contain more metals than any other known planet.

Eris *Moon* *Earth*

Pluto

▲ New planets have also been found in our own Solar System. **Eris** is an ice dwarf bigger than Pluto, but much further from the Sun. There may be even more to be found!

▼ The two smaller stars circle the big one, but from time to time the three line up. The scene here is set on a possible moon that circles the large planet.

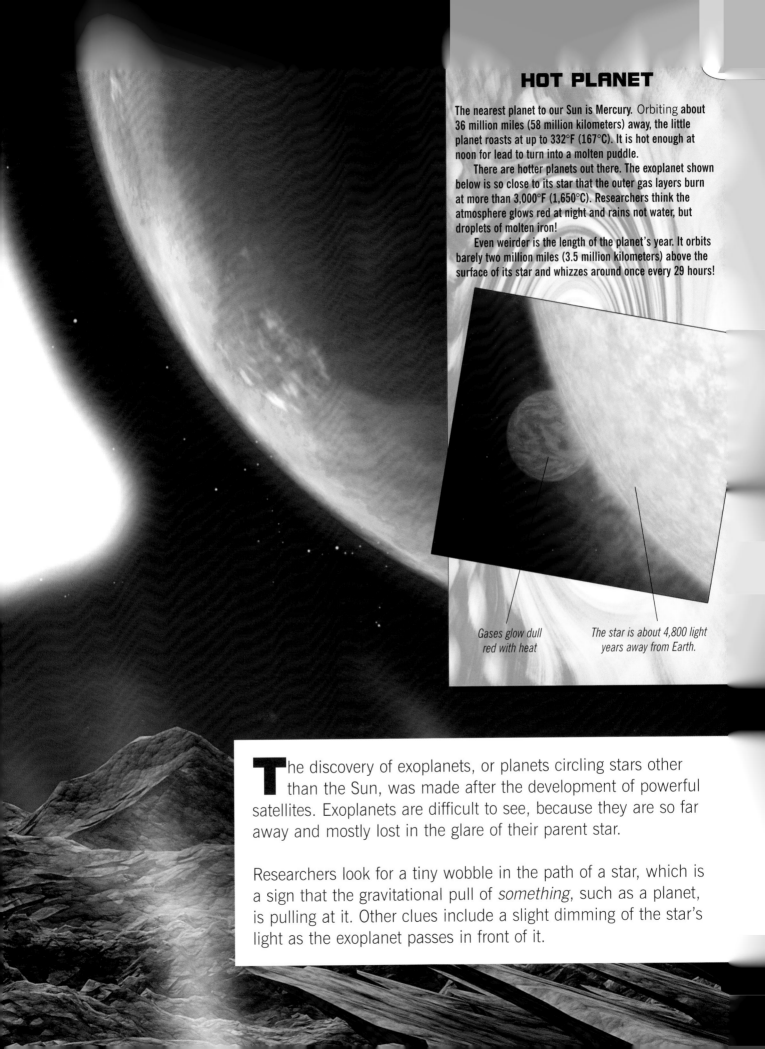

HOT PLANET

The nearest planet to our Sun is Mercury. Orbiting about 36 million miles (58 million kilometers) away, the little planet roasts at up to 332°F (167°C). It is hot enough at noon for lead to turn into a molten puddle.

There are hotter planets out there. The exoplanet shown below is so close to its star that the outer gas layers burn at more than 3,000°F (1,650°C). Researchers think the atmosphere glows red at night and rains not water, but droplets of molten iron!

Even weirder is the length of the planet's year. It orbits barely two million miles (3.5 million kilometers) above the surface of its star and whizzes around once every 29 hours!

Gases glow dull red with heat

The star is about 4,800 light years away from Earth.

The discovery of exoplanets, or planets circling stars other than the Sun, was made after the development of powerful satellites. Exoplanets are difficult to see, because they are so far away and mostly lost in the glare of their parent star.

Researchers look for a tiny wobble in the path of a star, which is a sign that the gravitational pull of *something*, such as a planet, is pulling at it. Other clues include a slight dimming of the star's light as the exoplanet passes in front of it.

DANGER IN SPACE!

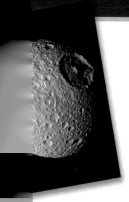

The universe is a deadly place, full of meteors and space rocks that can collide with planets and cause enormous explosions on impact.

▲ The space rock that made this crater on Mimas, a moon of Saturn, was huge. If it was just a little larger, it would have split Mimas into pieces.

Every day the Earth's atmosphere is bombarded with space debris such as **asteroids**, dust, and rock. Most of the debris burns up harmlessly before it can reach the Earth, but about a dozen fist-sized lumps hit the ground each day. Millions of years ago, huge chunks of space rock pounded Earth. Some scientists think the dinosaurs were killed off by a rock so large that the massive impact set off tidal waves and climate change.

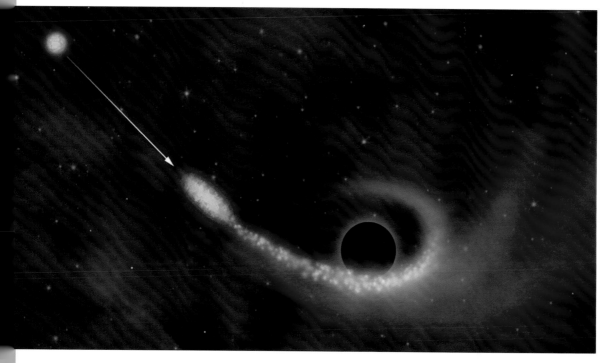

▲ The pull of gravity from a black hole rips apart a passing star.

▶ A collision in space near the star Vega, located 25 light years from Earth. Repeated smashes like this created a large rocky ring around the star.

Some experts think Earth should have a **radar**-warning system that alerts us when space rocks, or meteoroids are on a collision-course with Earth.

The force of a meteoroid's impact with Earth would blast a crater into the Earth's surface that is far greater than the size of the meteoroid. A major meteoroid hit would mean disaster.

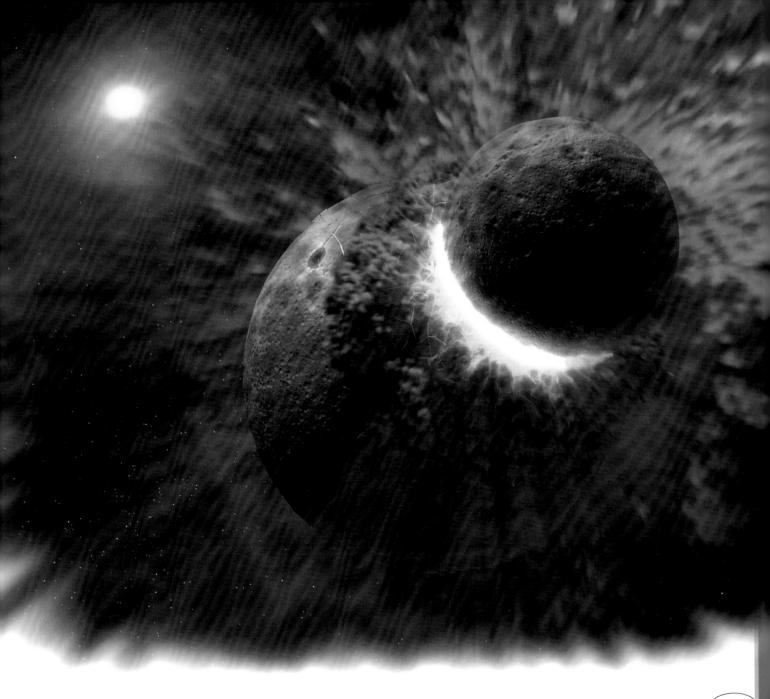

OUR DEADLY GALAXY

As far as we know, Earth is the only place in the Solar System where life – or at least, complex life such as ourselves – exists. This is because Earth orbits at a safe distance from the Sun. The planet is not too hot and not too cold for life. It looks as if the same is true for the Solar System's place in the Milky Way.

Researchers have found that the Solar System is cruising in a narrow band about two-thirds of the way from the center of the galaxy. This band is called the GHZ, or Galactic Habitable Zone, a place that is habitable, or suitable for life. If we were closer to the center, collisions with space debris and radiation would be too great. Further out in the Milky Way's distant outer zones, there may not be any planets with conditions like those on Earth.

Position of Earth

COMING SOON?

New space telescopes will peer deeper and deeper into space in the future. They will be looking for new planets, strange stars, and any signs of alien life.

▼ Here, distant exoplanets are imagined circling another star. The blue Earth-sized world is shown as a moon of a much bigger planet.

▲ The Kepler space telescope will search the skies for Earth-sized planets and for signs of life on them.

The main goal for researchers is to understand how the universe works and whether or not there is life on other planets. It seems unlikely that humans are the only intelligent life forms, but the search is still on. Deep space research is paying off. Just a few years ago, no one knew if there were any planets circling other stars.

Today we know there are hundreds of planets out there. We have not yet found any that are anything like the Earth, but with better telescopes, who knows what we will find.

Some scientists even think the Sun has a hidden companion star that could be a black hole. Only more research will help us find out!

▲ A new system of planets forms from a whirling ring of dust and rocks.

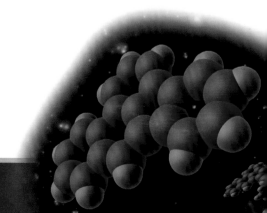

BLACK HOLE POWER?

Some scientists have proposed the idea of using black holes as power stations. They believe the black hole's massive gravitational pull could somehow be harnessed. Future experiments include designing an artificial black hole to study how it attracts energy. The laboratory black hole would be suspended by powerful magnets. It would have to be well protected or its gravity could suck in anything.

Some people think that one of today's advanced research systems, called the Large Hadron Collider (LHC), may have already created micro-holes, even if only for the briefest moments.

Science fiction author Charles Sheffield has written about a future where black holes are used for power.

One of the sci-fi books by Charles Sheffield.

Some of the LHC's equipment.

Telescopes that are planned for the future include the Kepler and James Webb instruments. They will help astronomers peer further into space than is possible with current equipment. One thing is certain – the universe is full of surprises and we will continue to find things that puzzle and amaze us.

▶ The molecules of life seem to be scattered throughout the universe – if so, then there may be life on many other worlds.

DISCOVERY TIMELINE

Astronomers have studied the skies for thousands of years, but we have only started to understand what is out there.

1608 Dutch lens-maker Hans Lippershey (1570-1619) perfects a design for the first telescope.

1609 Galileo Galilei (1564-1642) makes a telescope from Lippershey's plans. In 1610 he publishes the results of his work, which includes observations of the Sun and several planets and their moons.

1783 English geologist John Michell (1724-1793) determines that a star that was big enough would vanish from sight because light could not escape from it.

1796 French scientist Pierre Simon de Laplace (1749-1827) presents similar ideas to Michell, along with many other astronomical theories.

1830s Helix nebula is discovered by the German astronomer Karl Harding (1765-1834). The gas cloud is the outer remains of a Sun-like star exploding. The core has now shrunk to form an Earth-sized white dwarf.

1915 German astronomer Karl Schwarzschild (1873-1916) writes his pioneering work on black holes.

1923 U.S. astronomer Edwin Hubble (1889-1953) finds that our Milky Way galaxy is just one of many galaxies, scattered throughout the universe.

1957 The Space Age begins, with the launch of a small Russian satellite called Sputnik 1.

1963 New Zealander Roy Kerr (1934-) discovers that black holes can rotate, like most stars.

1967 First neutron star is discovered. It is a **pulsar**, a spinning neutron star that sends out powerful bursts of radio energy like a space lighthouse. Most neutron stars seem to be of this type.

1968 U.S. physicist John Wheeler (1911-) coins the term "black hole."

1969 On July 26, two astronauts of the Apollo 11 space mission touch down on the Moon.

1971 British physicist Stephen Hawking (1942-) shows that in the early days of creation, many mini-black holes were formed. His book *A Brief History of Time* (1988) includes a lot about black holes. It becomes an international best seller, with more than nine million copies sold.

▲ Hans Lippershey, designer of the first telescope.

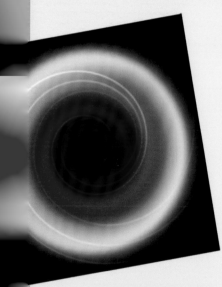

▲ As glowing gas spirals into a black hole, it dims gradually until it vanishes from sight at the event horizon.

1972 Cygnus X-1 is the first space object generally agreed to be a black hole. The discovery is made by researcher Tom Bolton, at the University of Toronto, Canada.

1981 Alan Guth (1947-) proposes the idea of cosmic inflation, in which he suggests that the early universe expanded like a balloon to the size it is today. In Guth's words, "the universe is the ultimate free lunch."

1983 The IRAS space telescope spots a ring of gas and dust around the star Vega. This could be a sign of another Solar System in formation.

1990 The Hubble space telescope is launched. It sends back thousands of pictures that show many wonders in the depths of space. The Hubble may be able to stay in working condition until sometime after 2010.

1991 The first planets of another star are found. There are two of them, circling a distant pulsar.

1997 The sci-fi movie Contact is released, featuring a wormhole system for travelling to distant areas of space almost instantly.

1998 The Hubble space telescope takes pictures of a firestorm of black hole formation in the Centaurus A galaxy, 10 million light years away.

1999 The Chandra x-ray telescope, named after the scientist Subrahmanyan Chandrasekhar

(1910-1995), an Indian-American who has done much research into white dwarf and neutron stars. Chandra also means moon in the ancient Indian language, Sanskrit.

1999 The XMM-Newton telescope is launched, named after the English scientist, Isaac Newton (1642-1727). XMM-Newton observations include hot spots on neutron stars and, closer to Earth, the comet Tempel.

1999 The nearest black hole to Earth is discovered. It is called V4641 and is about 1,600 light years away.

2000 Chandra's operation includes studies of Sagittarius A, a region of space at the core of our Milky Way galaxy. In it there is a black hole, which is about 2.6 million times more massive than the Sun.

2003 The Spitzer infrared space telescope is launched. In 2005, the 2,094 pounds (950 kilograms) instrument was the first to capture a visual image of an exoplanet.

2004 The Swift space telescope is launched to look for gamma-ray bursts (GRBs), huge flashes in deep space. One of Swift's early observations was two neutron stars crashing into each other.

2005 The Solar System's tenth planet is found, far beyond the previous most-distant planet, Pluto.

2006 Pluto is reclassified as a dwarf planet

▲ The James Webb space telescope is a powerful instrument due to be launched around 2011. It should partly replace the Hubble, which will have stopped operations by then.

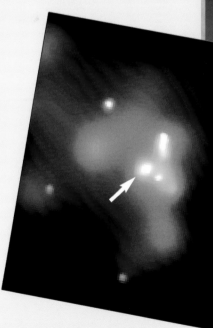

▲ A Chandra image of the Milky Way's core. The arrow marks the black hole that is thought to be there.

GLOSSARY

► The Crab nebula surrounds a pulsar, all that remains of a star that exploded in the year 1054.

An explanation of some technical words and concepts used in this book.

Accretion disk The ring of matter that spirals into a black hole.

Asteroid A rocky body in space.

Astronomer A scientist who studies the Solar System and the planets and stars in it.

Atmosphere The layer of gases that surround a planet.

Constellation A pattern or arrangement of stars.

Dense The parts that make up the matter or substance are closely packed together.

Elliptical galaxy A large group of stars and planets that are arranged in a variety of shapes.

Galaxy An enormous group of stars in a slowly rotating spiral, oval, or irregular shape.

Geologist A scientist who studies rocks and landforms such as mountains.

Gravity The force of attraction between objects. Massive objects have a stronger gravitational pull than smaller ones.

Hydrogen Lightest and most abundant gas in the universe.

Hypernova A huge explosion caused by an old star throwing off its outer layers.

Light year The distance that light covers in a year. It is about 5.9 billion miles (9.5 billion kilometers).

Nebula A glowing cloud of gas and dust in space. A planetary nebula is the remains of the outer shell of an old, exploded star.

Neutron star The collapsed core of a star that is larger than the Sun.

Nuclear fusion The process by which stars burn, in which hydrogen particles are fused, or joined in the intense heat and pressure found inside a star.

Orbit The curving path that one space body takes around a more massive one. The Earth goes around the Sun in a near-circular orbit that takes a year. The Moon orbits the Earth every 27.3 days.

Planet A large body that circles the Sun or another star. The Solar System has eight official planets, though some ice dwarfs may be big enough to be called planets too.

Pulsar A kind of neutron star that spins rapidly, sending out a flashing beam of powerful radio waves as it does so.

Radar An electronic system that sends out a radio beam using a transmitter. Solid objects reflect some of the radio energy back to the transmitter, which displays them on a TV screen as glowing blips showing their size, position, distance, and speed.

Radiation The range of wave energy in nature, from long radio waves to short gamma rays. Light is a part of this electromagnetic spectrum (EMS), about halfway between the extremes.

Singularity The area in a black hole where density is infinitely high. In a non-rotating black hole, this is a single point. In a rotating black hole, it occurs as a ring.

Solar panel Flat piece of material that converts the energy in sunlight to electricity.

Solar System The Sun and its planets, moons, and other space debris that circle it.

Star A hot, glowing ball of gas in space. The Sun is a medium-sized star – others may be bigger or smaller. Single stars are common, but so too are pairs of stars, called double-stars or binary pairs. There are even stars in groups of three or more.

Starburst galaxy Galaxy with an active core, probably due to stars being formed in a black hole zone.

Supernova Powerful explosions of burnt-out stars.

Trilobite A creature that was very common in the prehistoric seas about 250-520 million years ago. There were many kinds, large and small.

Ultraviolet rays Sunlight that can be harmful to people's eyes and skin.

White dwarf The collapsed core of a Sun-sized star, shrunken to a dense, hot object about the size of Earth.

Wormhole A tunnel between two points in space or time, thought to be created by a black hole's distortion of space.

X-rays Light beams that can pass through materials that regular light cannot pass through.

Year The time that a planet takes to circle its parent star once. On Earth, a year lasts for 365.25 days. Those planets that orbit nearer the Sun have shorter years, ones orbiting further away have longer years.

▲ This is NGC 253, a starburst galaxy some 12 million light years away. Many black holes are thought to be in the core zone of this galaxy.

WEB WATCH

The Internet is a good way to keep up with the latest information on black holes and space. These addresses are for very useful general-interest sites, which can lead you to more detailed information sources.

http://www.nasa.gov
This is the homepage of the space agency NASA, a treasure-trove of information on U.S. spaceflight.

http://hubblesite.org
The homepage of the Hubble space telescope, with pictures and information on the universe.

http://www.spitzer.caltech.edu
Homepage for another space telescope, the Spitzer instrument. Contains information about deep space and black holes.

http://www.space.com
A fascinating general-interest site for space stories, as well as a lot of pictures and videos.

http://www.spacedaily.com
Daily headlines on space with links that take you to the far corners of the Internet.

http://www.spaceflightnow.com
Another recommended space news site.

If you want more space stuff, then do not forget to use your school or local library. There are also many museums and special-interest exhibitions to look for. If you can visit a planetarium, the star displays are thrilling to watch.

INDEX

Acknowledgements

We wish to thank all those individuals and organizations that have helped to create this publication. Images were supplied by:

Airbus Industrie
Alpha Archive
Les Bossinas
CERN Geneva
Chandra X-ray Observatory
CXC/SAO
ESA European Space Agency
Goddard Space Flight Center
HST Hubble Space Telescope
R. Hurt
David Jefferis
JPL-Caltech
NASA Space Agency
Nissan Motor Co Ltd
T. Pyle
Aurore Simonnet
Sonoma State University
Swift Observatory
XMM-Newton

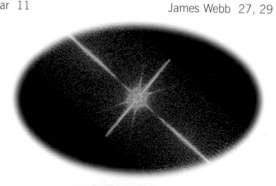